BAT 101-01-00 #1698

ULTIMATE
Cheerleading

By Kieran Scott

SCHOLASTIC, INC

New York   Toronto   London   Auckland   Sydney

To Wendy, Ally, and Shira.
Now, then, always, you're unbelievable!

ISBN 0-590-38651-4

Copyright © 1998 by Scholastic, Inc.
All rights reserved. Published by Scholastic Inc.

Produced by 17th Street Productions, a division of
Daniel Weiss Associates, Inc.
33 West 17th Street, New York, NY 10011

Cover design by Charles Kreloff
Interior design by Christopher Grassi

12 11 10 9 8 7 6 5 4 3 2 1   8 9/9 0 1 2 3/0

Printed in the U.S.A.

First Scholastic printing, September 1998

CONTENTS

Special Thanks

To Donna O' Reilly, St. John's University Cheerleading Coach, as well as her cheerleaders Keri Fiore, Cindy Arroyave, and Mary Greco.

We'd also like to thank the Pascack Hills High School cheerleaders who endured sunburned stunts, miniwrestlers, and hours of smiling to model for this book. They are, from top row, left, Aimee Molle, Maria Papazoglou, and Ani Manuelian. From middle row, left, Kristy Ingraham, Lauren Scott, and Jessica Tuve. From bottom row, left, Lynea Zbonack, Jacquelene Cutro, Erin Hult, and Lisa Garigliano. Thanks to their coach, Mary Beth Perry, and the PHHS faculty, staff, and administration for all their help.

ULTIMATE Cheerleading

READY . . .

O – K!

Chapter 1

Happy 100th!

Cheerleading Celebrates Its 100th Anniversary in 1998

Once an exclusive male privilege, task of producing ecstatic zizz-boom-bahs to encourage high school football teams now being taken over by lively misses. Do they inspire cheers? Well, look 'em over in action.

I know. You're thinking, "Huh?!!!"

But this is no joke. This is an actual headline from the *Newark Sunday Call*, dated November 20, 1932. One look at that outfit is enough to tell you that cheerleading has changed *a lot* over the years. And today, with ESPN televising competitions and companies like Nike and Adidas designing uniforms, the country is finally recognizing cheerleaders for what they are: athletes with great lungs.

It all started in 1898 at a University of Minnesota football game with a very spirited individual named Johnny Campbell. The legend is, good old Johnny realized his team needed a pick-me-up, so he got up and led his fellow students in a cheer. Soon after, he suggested that the school form a squad of six men to act as "yell captains." And so the first cheerleading squad was born.

A bunch of guys yelling chants like this:

Tah, rah, rah
Tiger, Tiger, Tiger
Sis, sis, sis
Boom, boom, boom
Aaaahhhhh!
Princeton! Princeton!
Princeton!

1

(Now, we owe a lot to our forefathers. But what does that *mean*?)

In the 1920s girls started to infiltrate cheer squads around the country. Seems guys realized girls were a lot easier to build and stunt with. And hey, they could be loud, too, thank you very much!

The year 1948 was a big one for cheerleading. Lawrence "Herkie" Herkimer (yes—the ever popular herkie jump is named for him) formed the first cheerleading camp to teach both the skills and the art of cheerleading. He also founded the National Cheerleaders Association—the first cheerleading organization. Today the NCA still offers camps and clinics and sponsors nationwide competitions. Wouldn't Herkie be proud?

Cheerleading reached its peak of popularity in the 1950s. Girls really took over for the first time. It all seemed to follow—Gidget, poodle skirts, and cheerleaders. It was a nice, pure, all-American thing for the teenage girl to do to support her male peers as they sweated it out on the field and on the court. Cheerleaders were often elected by the student body, not unlike homecoming or prom queens. You didn't really need all that much more than a pretty smile and a sunny disposition to make the squad.

Puh*leeze!*

Not anymore. The face of cheerleading is changing. Cheerleaders are athletes. They have to be strong enough to lift their own weight—sometimes above their heads. They have to be focused and coordinated enough not to drop each other or get dropped. They're gymnasts. They're dancers. They're stunters. They're cross trainers, choreographers, writers, artists, and organizers. They're graceful, strong, sharp, quick, energetic, tireless, and, above all, dedicated.

Now all they need is a little *r-e-s-p-e-c-t*. Some states have officially recognized cheerleading as a sport. And some, like Texas, Florida, Indiana, and Oregon, have gone the extra step to hold their own state championships as they would for football or basketball. But most states still refuse to call cheerleading a sport, deeming it an activity instead.

Like cheerleaders expend the same physical energy as the kids on the debate team or in the astronomy club. Sure. Okay.

The fight continues.

But it's a fight they're slowly winning, and you can do your part. If your school or organization doesn't recognize cheerleading as a sport, invite your principal to come to a stunting practice, or sit in on one of your all-day dance sessions, or check out your knuckles after you've practiced the basket toss for an hour straight—maybe even show them your biceps.

And if that doesn't work, simply ask—"Can your basketball players do this?"

CHEERLEADING IS ABOUT MOTIVATING OTHERS, BOTH THE TEAM AND THE CROWD. IT'S AN IMPORTANT TASK THAT CAN ONLY BE ACCOMPLISHED BY THOSE WHO GIVE IT ONE HUNDRED PERCENT.

—TYSON FERGUSON, MINNESOTA STATE UNIVERSITY

You've come a long way, baby!

Chapter 2

So You Want to Be a Cheerleader. . . .

. . . but which squad is right for you? Some schools have a bunch of different teams to choose from. Figuring out who cheers for which sports, which classes can cheer on which teams, and which squad fits your talents and interests can be as tough as your algebra homework. Squads vary from school to school, but here's a simple guide to go by:

Junior varsity cheerleaders

The JV squad is usually made up of freshmen, sophomores, and possibly juniors. This squad will cheer for junior varsity sports and may sometimes be asked to cheer at big varsity games to give the varsity squad extra support. While many junior varsity squads perform routines of the same complexity as the varsity team, others will stick to cheers and more basic building than the varsity.

Varsity cheerleaders

Usually made up of juniors and seniors, although some schools leave varsity open to sophomores as well. The varsity squad cheers for varsity games and matches. Some schools have separate squads for each sport: football, basketball, wrestling, and others. Varsity teams may also practice longer hours and work on more complicated skills than the other squads. Varsity squads often incorporate stunts, building, dance, and tumbling into their repertoire.

Freshman cheerleaders

Some schools have a separate squad for the fabulous frosh so that freshman sports teams have their own cheering section. The freshman squad is a great place to perfect your skills before you springboard onto the JV and varsity teams.

Pep squad

There are many definitions for a pep squad. It can be the band that plays in the stands at games and / or a group of students who promote spirit in the school. Often it's a group of aspiring cheerleaders who help with spirit events such as pep rallies, banner painting, or organizing spirit week. Some pep squads even join the cheerleaders on the sidelines or in the stands during big games.

Pom-pom squad/pom squad

Sometimes this is another name for the dance team, but while a dance team may not use pom-poms at all, the pom squad uses them for stunning visual effects during their routine. Pom squads often entertain on the sidelines during time-outs, working with the school band on short, peppy sequences. Coordination and a great smile are key.

Dance team

While some cheerleading squads perform their own dance routines during halftime and time-outs, some schools have a separate squad just for dancing. These girls are often trained in ballet, jazz, funk, and hip-hop. If dancing is your passion, the dance team is where you'll be able to shine.

Once you find out which types of squads your school sponsors, you can decide which squad is best for you . . . and which squad could best use you! If you're trained in dance and love to work on hip, fast routines, a dance or pom squad is probably right for you. If you're strong and loud, a cheerleading squad will give you an awesome workout doing stunts and jumps. If you just want to demonstrate your incredible school spirit and to see what cheerleading's all about from a more detached standpoint, check out the pep squad. No matter which team you choose and no matter where your tryout lands you, remember that you're there to support your team and your school, whatever your role may be.

The Big Day

You're sweating.

Your stomach is doing its own tumbling run.

Your heart is auditioning for the drum line.

Your hands are shaking, and your knees are nonexistent, and for some odd reason your scalp is tingling.

And now you're supposed to get out there and remember a cheer? Remember a dance routine? Remember how to pivot, how to execute the perfect cartwheel, and how to flash a mind-blowing smile?

Maybe, you think, I'd rather go home and rent a movie.

The best way to avoid a pretryout panic of titanic proportions is to come to tryouts prepared. Whether you have to audition in front of a few judges, the returning squad members, or the entire school, you have to show your audience that you're confident, poised, and happy to be there, even if the escape bus is calling your name.

PLAN AHEAD!

The best way to avoid freezing up or bailing out on tryout day is to be prepared. Most schools will hold a preliminary meeting for cheerleading hopefuls about a month before tryouts. But there are things you can do to prepare even *before* this meeting.

1. Watch the current squad

Going to games and checking out the cheerleaders will give you an idea of what will be expected of you during tryouts. You probably won't be asked to learn all their elaborate moves and complex stunts, but you will be asked to show the same enthusiasm, attitude, and energy. Also, if your squad does jumps or gymnastics on the sidelines, there's a good chance you'll be asked to demonstrate some ability in these areas. Once you know what you're in for, you can start practicing, stretching, and training right away.

2. Meet the coach

Find out who the coach is and introduce yourself. Tell him or her that you're interested in trying out for the squad and ask if there is anything you can do to prepare. Some coaches won't reveal anything because they might think it would give you an unfair advantage over other hopefuls, but the coach will now know how excited and dedicated you are, and he or she will remember your face.

3. Start training

If you're not in shape, get there. Cheerleading is an aerobic sport, which means you need a lot of energy and endurance. You can build up your strength with virtually any athletic activity you choose. Some good ones are: dancing, aerobics, swimming, running, and lifting weights. Also, do a lot of stretching. If you're limber and flexible, you'll be in perfect condition to try new stunts and tumbling runs. Besides that, you'll be safer—you have a much greater chance of getting hurt if your muscles are tight.

AT THE MEETING . . .

Pay attention. You'll find out when pre-tryout practices will be held, the date of the actual tryouts, what skills you will be expected to perform, and possibly even a dress code for tryout day. Listen to the coach and ask questions. Demonstrate your eagerness and dedication. Also, take note when you're told what your life will be like if you do make the squad. When and how long are practices? When are the games and competitions? If you can't give the squad one hundred percent, you should rethink whether or not you want to try out. Cheerleading is a big commitment of time and energy, so be ready to give it your all!

PRACTICE WEEK

1. Just do it

Keep your energy up, your head held high, and a smile on your face. Usually the current squad and the coach will be present at the practices. You have to make a good first impression. No whining. No "I cant's." Just keep trying and keep moving. Even if the cheerleaders and coaches aren't the ones to judge you on tryout day, you want them to know they can count on you if you make the squad.

> TWO-THIRDS OF ALL CHEERLEADERS ARE INVOLVED IN ANOTHER COMPETITIVE SPORT.

2. Work hard on your own time

Once you learn the routines, cheers, and/or jumps and gymnastics you'll need to perform, practice on your own as much as possible. Watch yourself in the mirror or practice with a friend to make sure your movements are sharp and correct. If you or a friend has a video camera, make a tape of yourself doing the routine. It may be agonizing to watch the first time, but it's a great way to reveal your trouble spots. And once you've identified your weaknesses, *focus* on them. If you've been faltering on your jumps, practice them the most. Don't avoid the elements that frustrate you. Conquering your weaknesses is the most gratifying kind of progress.

3. Dress for s-u-c-c-e-s-s

Chances are, if you know you look your best, you will perform your best. The last thing you want to worry about on tryout day is whether your sneakers are clean. Plan your tryout uniform ahead of time and you won't be standing there thinking, I should've ironed this shirt. They're staring at the wrinkles. Do my socks match? Oh, my gosh, I don't think they match! You'll be thinking, I am dressed to impress, and that is exactly what I'm going to do.

A few days before the tryout pick out your clothes and hang them up so you know where they are. (Yes, a few days. Because if you do it the night before, you will, without a doubt, discover that your best blue T-shirt was used as a painting smock by your little sister and your formerly crisp white shorts made it into the colored wash.)

Some schools will hand out a dress code at the pretryout practices. Adhere to it to the letter. If they want white socks for some unknown reason, wear them. If they want your hair up, put it up. Don't risk losing points over minor appearance issues, even if you do look better with your hair down.

YOUR MOMENT

1. Have fun!

Even if you're battling butterflies, you can still smile and enjoy yourself. Keep reminding yourself how hard you've worked and how much you want it, and the tryouts will fly by. Plus the judges will pick up on your enthusiasm, and your marks will undoubtedly jump.

2. Keep smiling

No matter what—even if you mess up—keep grinning and cheering. No one's perfect, and the judges will appreciate a good comeback from a flub as much as they'll appreciate a flawless performance. Don't forget, your job as a cheerleader is to get the crowd psyched, so look each of the judges in the eyes. Pretend those few judges are a crowd of fans, and do everything you can to get them cheering. Athletic ability and skill obviously count, but it's your energy, poise, and grace under pressure that they'll remember.

3. Be loud

This is one of the most important fundamentals of good cheerleading. Take deep breaths, yell from your chest rather than your throat, and keep a low voice—it's louder than a high-pitched, whiny one.

AFTER THE TRYOUT

Stay poised. If your coach calls everyone in to announce the new squad or posts the list in front of the rest of the hopefuls, keep cool. You don't want to shriek with joy two seconds before you realize your best friend didn't make it. By the same token, you don't want your tear dam to burst if *you* don't make it. There's always next time, and part of being a good sport is losing well. When you try out again, your coach will remember your grace and courage.

When you get home, rent Titanic and bawl all you want.

The Basics

Just like any other sport, cheerleading consists of a few basic skills you should learn before going on to bigger and more difficult routines. Most cheers and chants are performed by combining basic moves, or variations on them, along with the words themselves.

The most important thing to remember when learning these basic motions is to keep your moves sharp and precise. If you really hit your moves and if your squad is in sync, you'll give a fabulous performance.

Cheers are long routines that are performed during timeouts, the time between quarters in a basketball or football game, or between matches at a wrestling meet. They include elaborate moves and possibly some building or gymnastics.

Some cheers are mostly for entertainment value, but others may capitalize on crowd participation by using signs to bring the crowd into the cheer and cues to tell them what to yell and when.

Chants, also known as *sidelines,* are short cheers repeated three or four times to get the crowd into the game.

These are performed while the game is in play. During basketball games some squads even lead chants from the bleachers to really get the spectators into the spirit. Chants often use the same basic moves as cheers, but they may also just consist of rhythmic clapping and shouting.

Get psyched! Because once you've learned all the skills this chapter has to offer, you'll be ready to cheer with the best!

Voice and Expression

It can't be said too often: Keep your voice low and loud, and keep a smile on your face. If you yell from your chest rather than your throat, your voice will be naturally louder and will carry farther. And if you look like you're having fun, the crowd will have fun. Some squads even choreograph their expressions. A grin here, a little attitude there. It's up to you.

Claps

Yes, believe it or not, in cheerleading a clap is not just a clap. Most cheerleading squads today use only the *clasp* to keep the routine sharp.

Some cheers may still call for a regular *clap*. If so, make sure your hands are rigid and your clap is precise.

Don't bend your fingers at all or curl the fingers of one hand over the other.

Hands

There are five basic hand positions. With each of these positions there are two important things to remember. First, always keep your wrists rigid. If everyone on the squad bent their wrists in varying degrees, it would make for a sloppy performance. Second, when your hands are in fists, always keep your thumb on the outside. If you clasp your thumb on the inside of your fist, you risk straining the joint of your thumb.

Blades

Open your hand flat and make sure all your fingers are pressed together.

Daggers

Make a fist with the pinkie side facing out, as if you were holding a dagger.

Buckets

Make a fist with the thumb side facing out and your knuckles up, as if you were carrying a bucket.

Candlesticks

Make a fist with your thumb side facing up and your knuckles out, as if you were holding a candlestick.

Knockers

Make a fist with your thumb and knuckles facing out, as if you were about to knock on a door.

Arms

Hands on hips
Bend your arms and rest your hands just atop your hips. Make sure your hands are in fists.

Broken low V
Make a low V, then bend your arms at the elbows. Dagger fists.

High V
Bring your arms up into a V position. Remember to make sure your arms are stiff. Don't bend at the elbows. Your fists should be in buckets. Keep your wrists tight!

T
Extend your arms out straight from your sides. Hands are usually in buckets, sometimes candlesticks.

Low V
Bring your arms down into a V position. Stiff arms, tight wrists, bucket fists.

Broken T
Bend your arms at the elbows. Your fists should have the pinkie side facing out.

Broken high V
Make a high V, then bend your arms at the elbows. Your fists should have the pinkie sides facing out.

Vertical up (touchdown)
Bring your arms straight up above your head. Make sure your elbows are locked. Dagger fists.

Vertical down

Bring your arms straight down. The thumb side of your fist should be facing out.

L

Punch one arm straight up with the fist in a dagger. The other arm punches straight out to the side with the fist in a bucket. Your arms form an L shape.

Diagonal

Bring one arm up as if you were doing a high V, the other down as if you were doing a low V. Keep your arms straight. Bucket fists.

Punch up

Punch one arm straight up with the fist in a dagger. The other hand is at your hip.

Broken diagonal

Bend either the low arm or the high arm at the elbow.

Cross

Punch one arm across your chest with the hand in a bucket fist or a candlestick. The other hand is at your hip.

Punch out

Punch both arms straight out in front of you. Candlestick fists.

K

Bring one arm up as if you were doing a high V. The other arm punches down diagonally in front of your body.

Legs

Feet together

The basic starting position for most cheers. The insides of your feet should be touching. Make sure your shoulders are square and your back is straight.

Lunge left

Keeping your right leg straight, bend your left leg so that your knee is directly over your ankle.

Feet apart

Another basic starting position. Your feet should be about shoulder width apart.

Lunge front

Keeping the back leg straight, bend the front leg so that the knee is directly over the ankle.

Lunge right

Keeping your left leg straight, bend your right leg so that your knee is directly over your ankle.

Stag

Bring one knee up so that your foot is even with your other knee.

Now that you have all the basic hand, arm, and leg motions, you can mix them up to make up your own routines. Here are some basic ideas for mixing moves:

Starting a Cheer

There are a few ways to start off a cheer. Usually the entire squad will stand with feet together, hands on hips. The captain of the squad will call out the name of the cheer, then yell, "Ready!" Then the squad answers back, "OK!" Sometimes the captain will just yell, "Ready, OK!" him- or herself. If the squad decides on the cheer before they run out onto the court or field, there's no need to yell out the title of the cheer. It's up to your squad to figure out which method you're most comfortable with.

Crowd Participation Cheers

Crowd participation cheers are the most important routines you can perform. After all, you are a cheer*leader*. Your job is to get the crowd involved in the game—to help the spectators help the team! The following cheers use sharp, simple movements so that the crowd will concentrate on yelling at the right times instead of focusing on your fabulous skills. You might want to make large signs in your team's colors to cue the crowd. Poms also come in handy. Use them to point to the fans when they're supposed to yell.

Let's Go, Blue

R - V - H - S
Let's go, Blue!
R - V - H - S
Let's go, Blue!
Dolphin fans,
are you ready to cheer?
Let's go, Blue!
Let's go, Blue!
Let's go, Blue!

Go! Fight! Win!

Fans on the right yell *go!*
Go!
Fans in the middle yell *fight!*
Fight!
Fans on the left yell *win!*
Win!
Tiger fans, let's hear it
again!
Go! Fight! Win!

Spell It Out

Lions! Lions!
Let's spell it out!
L - I - O - N - S
Spell it again
L - I - O - N - S
Go, Lions!

Sidelines

Sidelines are short chants that are repeated three or more times. Movements are often simple, and some sidelines use only claps for rhythm. Following are ten sideline chants, most of which can be used for any sport. Use the basic moves you learned earlier and insert your mascot name, your team color, or your school name however you like. Once you see how simple a chant can be, you'll be off writing and choreographing your own in no time!

Score

S - C - O - R - E
Score! Score!
M - O - R - E
More! More!

Here We Go

Go!
Hey, here we go!
Tigers!
Go!

Show 'em Who's Best

C - O - W - B - O - Y - S
Cowboys! Cowboys!
Show 'em who's best!

Back to Basics

Back to basics,
Mustangs attack!
When the going gets tough,
The tough bounce back!

I LOVE TO GET OUT ON THE FIELD OR COURT AND DO THE BEST I CAN TO MAKE THE PLAYERS FEEL LIKE SOMEONE CARES. WHEN WE WIN A GAME, THE GREATEST FEELING TO ME IS WATCHING THE PLAYERS CELEBRATE.

—BRANDI HOUSE, KONAWA HIGH SCHOOL, ILLINOIS

Can't Be Beat

Ramsey fans, up on your feet!
Devils' spirit can't be beat!

We Are the Best

We are the best!
Bet you'll be impressed!
Owl fans stand up and yell
Better than the rest!

Sack That Quarterback
(Football)

Defense attack!
Sack that quarterback!

Attack

Let's go, Giants!
Attack!
Let's go, Giants!
Take that ball back!

Sink It In
(Basketball)

Let's go, Sharks!
Sink it in!
Let's go, Sharks!
We want a win!

You've got the moves, the words, the voice, and the smile. Now you're ready to get out there and share your spirit with the fans!

Chapter 4

Power Moves

Strength 101

Flexibility, strength, and endurance are the keys to cheering like a pro. Leading a healthy lifestyle is a must. If you're dedicated to cheerleading, you have to take care of yourself and keep in the best shape possible. Here are some tips to help you stay energized, avoid injury, and ensure a great performance.

STRETCHING

Always stretch your muscles before and after workouts, games, and competitions. This will help keep your muscles strong and help you avoid pulls and strains.

Butterfly stretch

Sit with your feet touching, your back straight. Pull your feet as close to your body as you can and press down on your knees with your elbows. Hold for fifteen to thirty seconds. Repeat.

Quadriceps stretch

Keeping your back flat, bend your leg behind you and grab your ankle. For a greater stretch don't lift your leg out or up higher, just keep your back flat. Hold for fifteen to thirty seconds. Repeat on other leg.

ALTHOUGH PRACTICE IS THE KEY TO SUCCESS, ATTITUDE IS EVERYTHING!
—DANI ROBBINS, HARRIMAN HIGH SCHOOL, NEW YORK

Pike stretch

Stand with your feet together, bend at the waist, and bring your face as close to your knees as possible. Hold for fifteen to thirty seconds.

For a greater stretch cross one foot over the other and hold. Repeat on other leg.

Straddle stretch

Stand with your feet apart, wider than shoulder length, and lower your body to one knee.

Next move your body to the middle and hold.

Then move to the other knee and hold. Hold each of these positions for fifteen to thirty seconds.

Arm stretch

Cross one arm in front of your body and use your hand to push it toward your chest. Hold for fifteen to thirty seconds.

Arm behind your head stretch

Lift one arm and bend it behind your head. Use the other hand to press down on your elbow. This will help the stretch. Hold fifteen to thirty seconds.

STRENGTH

When you build strength as well as flexibility in your muscles, you reduce the chance of injury. Standard strength exercises are familiar and not always fun, but they'll help you in the long run. Get ready to feel the burn!

Squats

Stand with your legs shoulder width apart, your back flat. Sit back, extending your arms forward. Don't sit back too far. If you can see your toes, you're in the right position. Now stand up, pulling your stomach in and your buttocks under. Do three reps of fifteen squats.

The Blockheads at the University of Illinois are the world's largest and oldest student cheering section. Over twelve hundred students perform intricate card stunts during halftime of every home football game.

Leg lifts

Lie flat on your back. Bend one leg and lift the other, keeping it straight.

Do ten lifts on each leg.

Next roll on your side, supporting your weight on your elbow.

Lift your leg about six inches, then lower. Repeat ten times on each leg. Make sure to keep your body rolled forward so your weight is on your hip, not on your buttocks.

Crunches

Lie flat on your back and bend your knees.

Place your hands behind your head and raise your chest about six inches off the ground, using your stomach muscles.

Do not pull your weight up with your hands, or you will strain your neck. Start with ten crunches and work your way up to fifty as you strengthen your abs.

ENDURANCE

Solid aerobic training will help you keep your energy up and keep you from losing your breath during your cheerleading workouts and performances. As stated earlier, almost any exercise that gets your heart rate up will help you keep up your endurance. On your days off from practice maintain your aerobic strength by exercising for thirty minutes. After your next practice or game, your heart will thank you.

WHEN EXERCISING, ALWAYS REMEMBER: MAINTAIN A STEADY PACE AND DON'T OVEREXERT YOURSELF. IF YOU FEEL FAINT OR SHORT OF BREATH, TAKE A BREAK OR SLOW IT DOWN.

LIVING HEALTHY

Staying in shape does not mean staying rail thin. A cheerleader needs to be strong, and that means maintaining a healthy, balanced diet. Crash dieting will result in a total body crash. You'll be tired and irritable and a liability to your squad. If you want to keep your body fat down and maintain your energy level, cut down on fatty foods and junk food. But don't cut down on your three square meals. Include all four basic food groups in your daily diet. If you eat well and work out hard, you'll maintain the athletic physique you're looking for.

So You Still Aren't Convinced that Cheerleading Is a Sport?

Cheerleaders and coaches across the country are trying to convince state, county, and school administrators that cheerleading is indeed a sport. The topic has been covered in newspapers, in magazines, on web sites, and on message boards. Meanwhile ESPN and NBC sports are televising competitions, cheerleaders are often spending more time working out than members of the recognized sports they cheer for, and studies show that more injuries result from the grueling athletic strain of cheerleading than from any other athletic activity.

Still not convinced?

Keep reading.

STUNTS

Stunt work is one of the most athletic tasks of the cheerleading squad. Both the bases (those who are climbed *on*) and the flyers, mounters, climbers, or tops (those who *climb* or are *thrown*) must be coordinated, brave, and above all, strong. Following are a few very basic stunts, broken down to help you learn the proper techniques. A word of warning—when performing stunts, always have an experienced coach or trainer present and always use a spotter. Techniques for stunts are very specific, and the correct form will keep you from seriously injuring yourself and your friends.

The Double Lunge or Thigh Stand

Mount:

(1) The two *bases* lunge toward each other, keeping their hips squared to the front. The *mounter* places her hands on the bases' shoulders and steps in one base's pocket. This *base* wraps her arm around the *mounter's* ankle.

Note: *There should be a strong "pocket" where your thigh meets your hip. Have the spotter push on your "pocket" to* make sure you're sturdy the first time you perform the stunt. Once you get the feel for the correct position, you'll be able to step right into it.

(2) The *mounter* then places her other foot in the other *base's* pocket. The other *base* wraps her arm around the *mounter's* ankle.

(3) The *mounter* stands up, locking her knees, arms raised in a high V.

(5) The *mounter* jumps down to the front. The *bases* stand straight.

DISMOUNT:
(4) The *mounter* grasps hands with the bases.

Dive rolls and thigh pitches are two stunts that have now been declared illegal by the National Federation of State High Schools Associations (NFSHSA).

The Pony Sit

MOUNT:

(1) The *base* bends her knees, with her feet about shoulder width apart, and braces her hands over her knees. The base should keep her back flat and rigid. The *mounter* places one hand near the base's shoulder, the other on the small of the base's back.

(2) The *mounter* hops into a sitting position on the base's back, supporting her weight with her arms as she jumps. The *mounter's* feet should be tucked in.

(3) The *mounter* raises her arms in a high V.

DISMOUNT:

(4) The *mounter* hops down as the *base* stands up straight.

The Shoulder Sit

MOUNT:

(1) The *base* stands in a lunge, creating a climbing pocket as directed above. The *mounter* places her foot in the pocket and her hands on the base's shoulders. The *base* should wrap her arm around the mounter's knee.

Note: Some mounters are more comfortable climbing on one side than the other. Try both to see which side suits you.

(2) The *mounter* stands straight and swings her free leg over the base's shoulder. The *base* should support the mounter by keeping her hold on the mounter's knee, then grasping just above the mounter's other knee as she sits. The *base* stands up straight, bringing her feet together or keeping them at shoulder width. The *mounter* tucks her feet behind the base.

DISMOUNT:

(3) The *base* should slowly bring her arms under the mounter's legs, one at a time, and grasp hands with the mounter. The *mounter* straightens her legs. The *base* quickly shrugs her shoulders with a quick thrust to help the mounter dismount off her back.

(4) The *mounter* should land with feet together.

The Shoulder Stand

MOUNT:

(1) The *base* stands in a lunge, creating a climbing pocket as directed above. The *mounter* places one of her feet in the pocket and her hands in the hands of her base. The *base's* arms should be extended above her head.

(2) The *mounter* pushes off the ground, locking her knee and placing her foot on the base's shoulder. The *base* should keep her arms locked and strong, and the *mounter* should put her weight on her arms.

(3) Keeping her weight on her arms, the *mounter* gently places her other foot on the base's other shoulder. The *base* releases the mounter's hands one by one, placing each hand behind the mounter's calves. As the *base* straightens her knees the *mounter* stands up straight, tightening her body for balance.

DISMOUNT:

(4) The *mounter* steps off the front as the *base* assists by catching the mounter at the waist. The *mounter* should bend her knees to soften the impact.

Double Base into Double Base Extension

MOUNT:

(1) The two *bases* face each other and bend at the knees. The *mounter* places her hands on the bases' shoulders.

FOR EXTENSION:

(3) The *bases* dip together for momentum and lift the mounter up above their heads, locking their arms. Make sure the mounter's feet stay shoulder width apart. The *mounter* remains rigid to keep her balance.

(2) The *mounter* hops up and the *bases* catch her feet in both hands, gripping the toes and heels of the mounter's feet. The *bases* stand together and bring their hands up to chin level. The *mounter* locks her legs and stands straight.

DISMOUNT:

(4) Together the *bases* bring the mounter back down, bringing their hands to chin level.

(5) The *bases* release the mounter and extend arms out for the cradle catch. The *mounter* kicks her legs to the front and bends into a pike position, allowing the bases to catch her.

Note: *A spotter is essential for this stunt. He or she should stand behind the mounter at all times and hold her waist during the mount and dismount.*

Once you've perfected these stunts, you can use them in cheers or dances. Plus you can mix them up and use your basic climbing skills to create pyramids. There are also many other, more complex stunts to be learned as your skills become more advanced. Here are some examples of higher-level stunting work:

Please do not attempt these stunts without the instruction of a trained professional.

Remember that stunts take a lot of practice and focus, but they're one of the most thrilling, crowd-pleasing parts of cheering.

JUMPS

Jumps add an element of excitement and energy to your sideline presentation. Not only do they show the crowd you're psyched for your team, but synchronized jumps are stunning when worked into dance routines and cheers. To perform these jumps well, you must have strong, toned, and well-stretched leg and stomach muscles. Warm up with lunges and leg lifts before jumping, and keep your stomach strong with crunches.

The Prep

The key to a high, well-executed jump is a good prep.

First, stand on your toes and raise your arms into a high V. Make sure your body is straight—back flat, shoulders back, chin up.

Next, swing your arms in front of your body and cross them. Bend your knees.

Next, swinging your arms up for added momentum, jump as high as you can.

Once you perfect your prep, you can move on to the different types of jumps.

Note: *The momentum of the jump must come from your legs. When performing these jumps, bring your legs toward your arms and chest. If you pull your chest down, your jump will be lower and your landing will be sloppy.*

The Tuck

Keeping your feet together, jump straight up in the air and bring your knees to your chest. Arms raise up into a high V.

The Herkie

Kick one leg out straight to the side, parallel with the ground. Bend the other leg and keep the knee facing downward.

As with stunts, always practice jumps with a spotter until you've mastered the techniques. The spotter should lightly hold your waist as you perform the jumps.

The Spread Eagle

Jump straight up and bring your knees out in a V. Keep your legs straight and point your toes. Arms raise into a high V.

The Toe Touch

If you're limber enough to do a split, you can probably do this jump. It's one of the most difficult, so make sure you're well stretched and warmed up before attempting it. Jump straight up with some extra power to your pop. Keep your chest and shoulders high. Your arms go straight out to your sides as you swing your legs straight up and touch your fingertips to your toes. Make sure your toes are pointed.

GYMNASTICS

For added variety and excitement many squads incorporate gymnastic skills into their cheers and dance routines. Everything from a basic cartwheel to more complex tumbling runs (a round off–back handspring–back tuck is one of the most popular) can bring energy and spark to any routine. But gymnastic skills can't be learned overnight, and they can't be taught by a book. If you'd like to take your cheerleading to that next level, seek out the coaching of a trained professional. If your school has a gymnastics team, see the coach and ask if he or she would be willing to help out. Or find a local gymnastics school and inquire about classes and clinics. Be ready to work hard. Perfecting gymnastics takes patience, poise, strength, courage, and trust in your spotter, but the end result is impressive and well worth the effort.

DANCE

While dance and pom squads are popping up all over the country, dancing is still a major part of being a cheerleader. Not only do certain cheers incorporate hip-hop and jazz-inspired moves, but many cheerleading squads perform halftime dance routines and numerous sideline dances during games. Often squads choreograph their routines themselves, and some even mix their own music. Here are some tips for creating a routine that will keep the fans in the stands at halftime instead of running off to buy dry popcorn and overcooked hot dogs.

1. The Music

Use music that will grab the crowd's attention. Obviously you want something upbeat with a powerful rhythm, but it should also be psych music—a tune that will get the crowd clapping and cheering and having a good time. Grabbing a new dance tune hot off the airwaves is always a good move, but there are also some time-honored classics for halftime groovin'. Check out ESPN's Jock Jams CDs. They're awesome collections of crowd-pleasing, blood-pumping hits. These tunes will be used to put the crowd in a winning spirit for years to come!

2. The Intro

At the beginning of your routine, do something eye-catching. A lot of squads like to start out with a pyramid or a stunt. A good basket toss always makes the crowd take notice. They'll know you're not messin' around. You're there to entertain.

3. The Routine

Mix it up. The best dances use moves drawn from all styles of dancing—hip-hop, jazz, modern, ballet—and anything else you think suits your style. Always keep your audience on its toes. Follow a series of complex, intricate moves in perfect sync or stagger the moves from one squad member to the next to create a domino effect. Incorporate jumps and stunts if possible, and change your formation throughout the dance. Energy is key, so have fun and keep your spirit up. Some fans think halftime is downtime—but with you on the field or court, it's *show time!*

So cheerleaders not only perform gymnastics (a sport so well recognized it's probably the most popular event of the Olympic Games), they also lift one another, throw one another, and dance with grace, skill, and attitude.

Not a sport? Not a chance.

Chapter 5

Keepin' It Real

Part of being a cheerleader is promoting school spirit. Not only are you responsible for supporting the team and keeping the crowd psyched during games, but it's up to you to keep the spirit alive all week and all year round.

There are many ways to keep your fellow students in the spirit during the school year (and we'll give you some fabulous tips for that later in this chapter), but what about your squad? How do cheerleaders keep their winning spirit alive nonstop? After all, constant pep can be draining, and smiling all the time goes against the very nature of teenage existence. On top of that, there's summer. It's not easy to keep that school spirit alive when the lounge chair and marathon soap opera sessions call.

Want to keep your squad psyched, in shape, and raring to cheer?
Read on.

Camps

Cheerleading camp is the ultimate summer pick-me-up. They've been bringing squads from across the country together for over fifty years. Not only are camps an opportunity to learn new skills from trained professionals, but they give you a chance to train with squads you might never otherwise meet. You'll get to see what squads from other parts of the nation are doing, share your favorite routines, and establish bonds that will last a lifetime.

Summer camps also give your squad a jump start on training for the fall. Often squads are brought together in the spring and new members are added to the team. At camp you get the chance to learn about one another, work together—possibly for the first time—and get some serious squad spirit going.

Spending full days and full weeks together can teach you a lot about your teammates!

Ask any cheerleader what camp did for her, and one of the first things you'll hear is, "It taught us to work together as a team." When unity reigns, there's nothing your squad can't accomplish.

There are all kinds of camps to choose from, offered by the many national and international cheerleading organizations. Some of these organizations offer sleep-away camps at college campuses, some offer commuter or day camps, and others offer private camps—sending their instructors to your school to work specifically within your needs. Following is a list of cheer organizations and a quick overview of the benefits of each camp.

AMERICAN CHEERLEADING FEDERATION (ACF)
800-803-4294
WWW.CHEERACF.COM

The American Cheerleading Federation runs private and residential camps, and their instructors work within your squad's ability level. Pyramids, stunts, cheers, chants, jumps, tumbling, full dances, and tips for choreographing your own routines are included.

AMERICHEER
800-966-JUMP
WWW.M8.COM/AMERICHEER/

Americheer offers residential, commuter, and private camps that include specific classes in gymnastics and cheerleading at the squad's request so you can work on your weakest areas. All-star tryouts are held at each camp, giving the winners the chance to participate in the Citrus Bowl.

CHEERLEADERS OF AMERICA (COA)
800-252-4337 (800-25-CHEER)
WWW.COACHEER.COM

Cheerleaders of America's resident and private camps are open to peewee teams on up through high school for both building and nonbuilding squads. Cheers, chants, stunts, pyramids, and competition tips are all covered, and instructors offer daily evaluations. Bids are given for the COA national championships. Individual "Dream Team" qualifiers are eligible to participate in collegiate bowl game performances.

CHEER LTD.
800-477-8868
WWW.OLDMP.COM/CHEERLTD/

Cheer Ltd. comes to your school for a one-day clinic that focuses on the needs of your squad. Cheers, chants, dances, stunts, tumbling, and spirit tips included.

NATIONAL CHEERLEADING ASSOCIATION (NCA)
800-NCA-2-WIN
WWW.GOTEAM.COM

At NCA's commuter and resident camps professional instructors teach cheers, chants, dances, and partner stunts and hold classes for captains and coaches. They also have a special program called "Bleacher Mania" that will teach your squad everything you need to know about running a spirit-full pep rally. Teams are given the chance to qualify for the NCA national championships.

WHEN I TRIED OUT FOR THE SQUAD MY FRESHMAN YEAR, MY TWO BEST FRIENDS MADE IT AND I DIDN'T. IT KILLED ME TO SEE THEM WALKING AROUND IN THEIR UNIFORMS ON GAME DAY. BUT I KNEW I HAD DONE WELL AT TRYOUTS. THEY WEREN'T THAT MUCH BETTER THAN ME. SO I WENT BACK AND TRIED OUT AGAIN IN THE FALL AND MADE IT. THREE YEARS LATER I WAS NAMED CAPTAIN OF THE SQUAD. IMAGINE IF I HAD NEVER TRIED AGAIN?

—MELINDA CHASE, REGENCY HIGH SCHOOL, TEXAS

UNITED CHEERLEADING ASSOCIATION (UCA)
800-328-5618 OR 888-CHEER-UCA
WWW.VARSITYSPIRIT.COM

United Cheerleading Association offers many different summer camps as well as special one-day spring clinics to get your new squad going or to offer tips for cheering for spring sports. Summer camps are held in all fifty states and in countries around the world. They include instruction in cheers, sidelines, gymnastics, and stunts and competition tips.

UNITED SPIRIT ASSOCIATION (USA)
800-886-4USA
WWW.USACAMPS.COM

United Spirit Association offers camps for cheerleaders, song leading, mascots, color guard, and dance. Not only do their instructors work with you on cheers, stunts, pyramids, and safety, but they also provide game-action training. This program helps you learn the game and know when to cheer and primes you on crowd communication—important skills for any cheerleader.

WORLD CHEERLEADING ASSOCIATION (WCA)
888-TEAM-WCA
WWW.WORLDCHEERLEADING.COM

World Cheerleading Association offers resident, commuter, and private cheer and dance camps. Cheers, conditioning, dance, partner stunts, and pyramids are all part of the curriculum. Exceptional squads are awarded bids to the WCA national competition.

As you can see, you've got a lot of opportunities to choose from, so don't let them slip through your fingers! Camps are educational and challenging, but most of all, they're inspirational—and they'll keep you cheering straight through the summer!

A Magazine to Cheer About

For years there have been specialized magazines for everything from needlepoint to paint ball, from golf to gardening, but it wasn't until 1995 that cheerleading got its very own glossy, full-color, find-it-on-any-newsstand magazine. *American Cheerleader* is stuffed with competition information, safety tips, stunt work, style tips, fund-raising ideas, uniforms, cheers, and much more. They even hold a Cheerleader of the Month competition, the winner of which is featured on the cover of the mag. It's a page-turner! (For more info on the magazine write to *American Cheerleader*, 250 W. 57th St., Suite 1701, New York, NY 10107. Or check out their web site at www.americancheerleader.com)

Spirit 24/7

So now your squad is pumped up and ready to cheer, but what about the rest of your school? At many schools spirit runs rampant, but what can you do when a team is on a losing streak or a student body is just plain apathetic? As a cheerleader it's your job to show your fellow students how much fun cheering the team on and supporting the school can be. The key is to be creative, be spontaneous, and always show your pride.

Turn your school into a year-round pep rally. Okay, maybe it's not such a good idea to keep everyone cheering in the halls between classes, but you can remind them there's something to cheer for. Have your squad paint banners for every game. You can do this at the beginning of the season so the banners will be ready when needed, and it's a great bonding experience for your squad. Some schools have a pep club that gets involved with painting banners and creating other spirit paraphernalia. If so, great! The more the merrier when it comes to school spirit.

Hang the banners up in the gym, at the front of the school, or in the cafeteria, where everyone is sure to see them. On game day wear your uniforms to school, set up a face-painting booth before the game so fans can wear their spirit head to toe, decorate your cars, and decorate the team members' lockers. When the students see their colors everywhere, they're sure to get psyched for the game.

Pep rallies are key to school spirit. Not only does your squad get to run the show and hold the spotlight, but your school gets the satisfaction of hearing every single student cheer together. Some schools hold pep rallies before the big rivalry games, and others hold them before every match. After a successful pep rally the fans carry their spirit straight into the game-time stands.

Many cheerleading squads hold fund-raisers for new uniforms, to earn money to enter competitions, or for charities and other worthy causes. But a fund-raiser can also raise spirit. Sell school bumper stickers, footballs, or pom-poms. There are plenty of printers and uni-form catalogs that sell these items in bulk, so the prices are perfect for resale. Not only will

you raise money for your squad, but your efforts will benefit the school. When team members are constantly reminded of the number of people behind them, they'll undoubtedly play their hardest.

There are plenty of other ways you can contribute to a spirit-filled school atmosphere. Just brainstorm with your squad, and you'll come up with plenty of ideas that are right for your school. Keep the creative juices flowing, and you'll help make your school experience rich and memorable for everyone.

Basketball season can get pretty long, and people start to get tense from spending so much time together. We always make a point of having a midseason sound off where everyone gets to vent their frustrations. Usually we find out everyone is mad at their boyfriends or their parents or their teachers and not at the rest of the squad. Then we can help support each other and get back to the fun of cheerleading.

—Patricia Abrams, Morristown High School, New Jersey

Chapter 6

The Ultimate Triumph

Cheerleading used to be all about helping the football team win or letting the basketball team know the school was behind them. Today cheerleaders have another role to fulfill. They have competitions of their own to win. It's time for those traditional athletes to turn around and root for them!

Cheerleading and dance team competitions are held throughout the country and all around the world. All types of squads are invited to compete at many levels, from local to national, and in many different categories.

For example, the UCA championships, which are nationally televised each year on ESPN and ESPN2, encompass a number of title opportunities, including Junior High, Freshmen, JV, Varsity Nonbuilding, Small Varsity Coed, Large Varsity Coed, Small Varsity, Medium Varsity, and Large Varsity. In addition, UCA has partner stunt events, allowing a few members of the squads to win trophies specifically for their stunting skills. That gives schools a lot of opportunities for glory, and UCA is just one of many organizations that run competitions.

Like in any other sport, preparing for cheerleading competitions takes dedication, hard work, and some serious spirit. But cheerleaders who have had the chance to participate in these contests will tell you it's all worth it. If your squad decides to compete, not only will you get the chance to show your stuff in front of squads from around your district, state, or country, but you'll make memories that will last a lifetime. Preparing for competitions is a ton of hard work, but working toward a win is indescribably exhilarating. It brings a squad together like nothing else can.

The Indiana University Cheerleading Squad performing in the 1998 College Cheerleading National Championship.

Preparing for Competition

The first step, of course, is to find out about local or regional competitions and determine which you might like to compete in and which event your squad is right for. Most of the national cheerleading organizations mentioned in the camp section of this book hold national competitions. But the qualifying criteria are different for each. In some cases squads may qualify only if they attended the camp and were recommended by their instructor. Others allow squads to enter by submitting a videotaped performance. Still others only allow bids to nationals via regional competitions. Call the organizations to learn more about their criteria.

Of course, there are also local and state competitions held all over the country. For local, district, and county meets squads often need only register. These competitions then serve as qualifying matches for the state competitions. Again, the rules and criteria vary, so look into your state or county's policy.

Once you've decided to participate or have been invited to take part in a competition, you have your work cut out for you. First, you'll need to study the rules for that particular competition. Usually you'll be supplied with a guidebook that dictates everything from hairstyles and uniforms to building height and cheer length. Make sure each member of your squad studies the rules. Defying the rules may result in loss of points or complete disqualification. All your hard work may be ruined before you ever get to compete.

You may be expected to perform one or more cheers, a cheer and a dance, or just a dance or halftime routine. Some competitions put restrictions on building and stunts, and most have time limits. Again, make sure you know what the judges expect and modify your routines to fit the criteria.

Pom-poms were introduced in the 1960s. They were originally made of paper.

Creating the Routine

Once you've determined the type of routine you'll be performing, it's time to choreograph and perfect your moves. If you are under time pressure, you might want to work on a routine you've already been performing. Take a favorite cheer and add some elements to turn it into a real crowd pleaser. If you have a cheer in which you build but the competition doesn't allow stunts or pyramids, make up some creative new moves to take the place of the building. If you have more time, you might want to come up with a routine specifically for the competition.

Whatever you decide, once you commit to compete, practicing that routine becomes a major priority. Of course, unlike other team sports, cheerleaders continue to have all the regular responsibilities that go along with their sport. While preparing for competitions, cheerleaders still have to attend school matches, organize pep rallies, and keep the school's spirit high. Often squads schedule extra practices to focus specifically on the competition routine.

LEFT: Northern Kentucky, the squad that placed third in the 1998 College Cheerleading National Championship Division II Team Category.

RIGHT: Two-time team champion Kentucky Wildcats, winners in 1997 and 1998, perform a difficult toss routine.

Tips from the Judges

Cheer competition judges focus on a number of different elements, from appearance and showmanship, to difficulty of stunts, jumps, dance, and gymnastics, to the performance as a whole. Here are some tips on scoring big with the panel of judges.

1. Keep the difficulty level high, but don't try to perform beyond your abilities.

Judges at most competitions do rate elements based on their difficulty. A slight flub in a difficult stunt may even score higher than a perfect simple stunt. But trying to perfect a bunch of skills for a competition when you've never done them before can create a lot of pressure and even more mistakes. It's better to introduce only one or two new elements into a routine you know you can rely on. Your confidence will shine through.

2. Include all the required and/or allowed elements.

Just like in figure skating, cheerleading judges can mark you down if you don't perform required elements. For example, some guidebooks state that a cheer must include at least three different jumps. No amount of skill can make up for a failure to execute the compulsories and execute them well. Some competitions may list skills that are allowed but not required. Try to work in all the acceptable skills. The more variety and ability you demonstrate, the better you'll fare.

3. Be creative.

Judges have been to dozens of these competitions. Some have even competed themselves. Don't bore them. Mix it up and show them you've put thought and time into the choreography. Make your routine unique, and you'll catch their attention.

4. Pay attention to the basics.

When you're working on a complex routine, it can be easy to overlook the fundamentals. Judges score you on your motions. That means keeping your arms straight, moving your hands in sync, making sure your timing is right on. Keep formation changes swift and the routine flowing. Also, remember that even in competitions, you're cheerleaders. You'll be judged on your appeal to the crowd, so work on facial expression and vocal projection. Keep the spirit going and the energy high and make the audience cheer.

5. Make sure your appearance is neat and your uniforms are clean.

There's no need to distract the judges with mismatched uniforms or wild hair and make-up. Keep it simple. Don't wear jewelry, and make sure everyone in your squad has her hair back and is wearing minimal makeup. Some competitions will allow face paint or glitter if it's part of your regular uniform, but make sure to check the rule book before you decide on these and other accessories. As in try-outs, there's no need to lose points over appearance.

The North Carolina State University Wolfpack Cheerleading Squad, fourth in the 1998 College Cheerleading National Championship Division 1A.

Nationals

Making it to a national competition is an incredible triumph. Not only are cheerleading squads from around the country brought together for a huge, spirited party, but squads are given the opportunity to bring their schools into the national spotlight. What better way to show your school spirit than to have your hometown's name on the lips of viewers in all fifty states?

But even though national competitions are held in fun locales like Walt Disney World, Universal Studios, and Myrtle Beach, the road to nationals is not all fun and games. First, squads usually need to beat out the competition at local, district, and/or regional meets. Then there's the issue of raising money for the trip. Squads have to pay for travel expenses, which often include airfare and hotel accommodations as well as meals. Most squads also purchase new competition uniforms and poms to look their best onstage. All of this expense means a lot of fund-raising and a lot of penny-pinching.

Meanwhile, championship-level squads practice countless hours while still cheering for their teams and keeping up with their studies, chores, and social lives. It takes incredible dedication, but it can be an unforgettable time in your life. And even if your squad doesn't win, the experience of coming together with hundreds of people dedicated to excellence in cheerleading makes it all worth it. The level of spirit, excitement, and anticipation at national cheerleading competitions is in a league of its own. After all, the audience is full of cheerleaders. Talk about a loud crowd!

The Kentucky University Wildcat cheerleaders pose in the winner's circle after the 1998 College Cheerleading National Championship Division 1A.

National Competitions— Where and When

Here are the projected dates for national competitions held annually by cheerleading organizations and associations. All dates and locales are subject to change, so please contact the organizations for more details.

Americheer (800-966-JUMP)

March 1999 in Orlando, Florida

Competitions for junior high, high school, all-star, and dance squads. Also hold competitions for outstanding individual cheerleader. Registration for finals is open to all cheer and dance squads. Individuals must qualify at a regional competition or send in a videotaped performance.

COA (800-25-CHEER)

March 1999 in Myrtle Beach, South Carolina

Competitions for youth through high school squads. Also hold individual and partner stunt competitions. Squads and individuals must earn a bid to nationals at a COA camp.

NCA (800-NCA-2-WIN)

December 1998 through April 1999

Competitions for high school, all-star, dance, and college squads. Also hold competitions for group stunts at the high school level and partner stunts for the all-star and college squads. Squads may qualify at camp, at regionals, or by sending in a videotaped performance. The deadline for videos is in early October. The 1998 high school championships were televised on the USA Network, and the college championships were televised by CBS Sports.

UCA (800-328-5618 or 888-CHEER-UCA)
January through March 1999 in Orlando, Florida

Competitions for dance, junior high, high school, and college squads. Also hold partner stunt competitions. Squads must qualify at UCA regional competitions. The nationals are televised on ESPN and ESPN2.

WCA (888-TEAM-WCA)
December 1998 in Nashville, Tennessee

Competitions for high school and all-star squads. Squads may qualify at summer camp, at regionals, or by sending in a videotaped performance. Tapes are due in mid-November.

The Kentucky 'Cats championship season was helped along by a tough crew of men.

Cheerleading in College

Want a chance to travel around the country for free? Want front-row seats to the most exciting basketball and football games? Want to see your very own face on national television? No problem. All you've got to do is make the squad.

College cheerleaders go beyond the call of duty to promote school spirit. While some students have a hard time juggling academic responsibilities, living on their own for the first time, and making an entirely new set of friends, college cheerleaders add another huge time consumer to their daily lives. But they have fun doing it!

For many hopefuls, cheering in college is a whole new world. A lot of high schools don't allow their squads to perform stunts or gymnastics, but at the college level these skills are almost universal. Don't worry. You can still make the squad if you don't have these skills, but be prepared to work hard to perfect them quickly. During halftime at basketball games the opposing cheerleading squads often compete with each other as hard as the teams during game time.

Fantastic stunts and routines inspire incredible crowd participation, and the team that draws the most noise is the happy victor.

Cheerleaders in most NCAA divisions travel with the teams and follow a grueling practice schedule. Homework on the road and extra-credit projects for missed class time often become routine. But it's not all work. Cheerleaders often get to know the other squads in their division well, and sometimes teams work together to perform stunts or rivalry skits for the crowd. And it's all worth it when you find yourself cheering under the bright lights of Madison Square Garden in New York City or on the sidelines at the Hula Bowl in Hawaii. What a way to support your team!

Many colleges and universities across the country offer scholarships to cheerleaders, as they do for other sports. To find out more, contact the athletic department at the school to which you're interested in applying.

49

Real Men Cheer

Chicks in short skirts? Tell that to this guy. . . .

More and more guys are cheerleading in high school, but the real surge of men in cheerleading has come at the college level. Many colleges are more open to stunting and building than a lot of high schools, and these are the skills that allow men to shine.

Of course, it's never easy for guys. Some girls get mocked for cheerleading because people say it's silly or pointless, so imagine the slamming that guys endure. They're called everything from sissies to wimps to rah-rahs. Male cheerleaders not only have to work just as hard as the women to learn routines, chants, stunts, and gymnastics—they often have to do it under severe personal attack.

So why do they do it? A few good men give a few good reasons:

"Nobody believes it, but this sport is just as challenging as football. I quit the football team to cheer because it looked like a lot more fun. I was right."

—*Dominic Marco, Washington High School, Texas*

"Whenever one of my friends mocked me, I reminded him that I got to hang with some of the coolest girls in school every day and they were literally climbing all over me. More guys tried out the following season."

—*Doug Hiller, Emory University, Georgia*

Some guys even make a career out of cheering. Here's a tip from one of the pros:

"I would lose my voice, get kicked in the face on a daily basis, and spend half my time training. I've never had a better time!"

—*Ian Scott, Seton Hall University, New Jersey*

"If you have heard your music at a different competition, don't use it. Chances are that the judges will have heard it over and over again. Be creative. Get old music. Get movie sound tracks. Be original. Also, you may not realize how important the right smile is to a judge. Try to teach your squad to practice with a smile. Smile genuinely and have fun!"

—*Steve Sollitto, Boston College coach and National Cheerleading Association judge*

Cheerleaders or not, boys will be boys!

You're in Great Company

Cheerleading is as much about performance as it is about athletics. The stage presence and poise you perfect on the court can take you far once your cheering days are over. Check out these successful ex-cheerleaders.

Sandra Bullock

Sandra must have learned to perfect that beautiful smile on the sidelines. The ever popular actress from *Speed* and *While You Were Sleeping* was first an ever popular cheerleader at Washington-Lee High School in Virginia.

Courteney Cox

Monica Geller, Courteney's character on the hit TV show *Friends,* is one optimistic chick. Maybe Courteney learned to play peppy on the sidelines as a middle school cheerleader in Birmingham, Alabama!

Jamie Lee Curtis

The star of *True Lies* recently told E! Entertainment Television that she loves watching the nationals on ESPN. As a former cheerleader for Westlake School in L.A., she can certainly appreciate them.

Kirsten Dunst

Before she started cheering on her eighth-grade squad, Kirsten hit stardom in films like *Little Women* and *Interview with the Vampire.* Maybe she can share some star-quality poise tips with her squad!

Sally Field

This Oscar winner's first big-time role was as a peppy teenager on the television version of *Gidget*. She undoubtedly showed the same energy on the sidelines for Birmingham High School in Van Nuys, California.

Calista Flockhart

Calista (bottom row, third from left) cheered at Shawnee High School in Medford, New Jersey, before working on Broadway. In 1998 she went on to win a Golden Globe Award for best comedic actress for Fox's breakthrough comedy *Ally McBeal*.

Vivica A. Fox

Vivica shot to stardom in the summer of 1996 when she starred opposite Will Smith in *Independence Day*. But if you take a look at her resume, her success isn't surprising. Vivica was an all-around active student and cheerleader in Indianapolis, Indiana.

Teri Hatcher

Long before we were cheering Dean Cain on to win Teri's heart in *Lois & Clark, she* was warming fans' hearts as a cheerleader in Sunnyvale, California (Teri is the one down front).

Susan Lucci

This soap opera diva plays one of the most wicked women on daytime television. But before the writers of *All My Children* turned her into Erica Kane, she was a sweet-as-honey cheerleader in Garden City, New York.

Steve Martin

Known for his special brand of physical antics and show-stealing humor, Steve (far right) always loved being in the spotlight. He was a yell leader at Garden Grove High School in Garden Grove, California.

Madonna

The ultimate entertainer, Madonna (in the middle) has always incorporated elaborate dance routines into her stage shows. But one of her first dance gigs was as a cheerleader and dancer at Rochester Adams High School in Detroit, Michigan.

Rita Wilson

Before she starred in *Jingle All the Way* with Arnold Schwarzenegger and before she met and married Tom Hanks, this actress was a high school cheerleader. One of her first acting roles was as a cheerleader who beat Marcia Brady for a spot on the squad on *The Brady Bunch*.

Alicia Silverstone

This blond beauty didn't have to train too hard for her acrobatic role as Bat Girl in *Batman and Robin*. Alicia (bottom row, third from left) was already in top shape from her time as a JV cheerleader at San Mateo High School in California.

Renee Zellweger

Renee (second from left) stole hearts all over the world in *Jerry Maguire*, but first she stole the show with her gymnastic talent as a cheerleader in Katy, Texas.

Bruce Willis

Okay, so he wasn't an actual cheerleader, but we couldn't resist sharing that this tough guy, famous for action-packed roles in the *Die Hard* series of films, was voted Most School Spirited at Penns Grove High School in New Jersey.

Gimme a T! Gimme a V! TV Cheerleaders

Marcia Brady— The Brady Bunch

Cordelia Chase— Buffy the Vampire Slayer

Kelly Kapowski— Saved by the Bell

Claudia Salinger— Party of Five *(Well, she was a mascot, anyway)*

Brittany Taylor— Daria

You've Got the Spirit

Whatever your skill level, cheerleading can be an exhilarating and rewarding experience. You have the opportunity to participate in the triumphs of the teams you're cheering for and know that you had a hand in each victory. You form friendships with fellow students you might never have known if not for the bond of cheerleading. You work out hard, keep yourself in shape, and have fun doing it. You pump up the crowd, raise spirit at your school, and keep people smiling and entertained. You take the spotlight and gain confidence, poise, and pride. You may even bring home a trophy of your own to reflect all your hard work. But even if you never compete, you can take pride in the daily victory of your dedication, achievement, and, of course, spirit.

Now get on out there and *cheer!*

Photography Credits

Cover
Handelman, Dorothy

Back Cover
top right—Perry, Chuck
bottom right—Black Box / Index
    Stock Photography, Inc.
left—Coyle, David

Front Matter
p. i—Handelman, Dorothy
p. ii—Seth Poppel Yearbook
    Archives, Inc.
p. iii—Handelman, Dorothy
p. iv—London, Robin G.
p. v, top left—S. W. Production /
    Index Stock Photography, Inc.;
    top right—Losh, Bill / FPG
    International Corp.; bottom
    left—Coyle, David; bottom
    right—Black box / Index Stock
    Photography, Inc.
p. vi, Clockwise from top left—
    Coyle, David; center—Black
    Box / Index Stock Photography,
    Inc.; top right—Perry, Chuck;
    bottom right—Perry, Chuck;
    bottom left—Coyle, David

Chapter 1
p. 3—Coyle, David

Chapter 2
p. 4, left—Kaye, Allan / Index Stock
    Photography, Inc.
p. 4, top right—Perry, Chuck
p. 4, bottom right—Krasowitz,
    Michael / FPG International Corp.
p. 5, top left—Coyle, David
p. 5, bottom left—Perry, Chuck
p. 5, top right—Perry, Chuck
pp. 6–7—Perry, Chuck
p. 8—S. W. Production / Index
    Stock Photography, Inc.
p. 9—Perry, Chuck

Chapter 3
p. 10—Krasowitz, Michael / FPG
    International Corp.
p. 11—Matarazzo, Paul
pp. 12–14—London, Robin G.
p. 15—Daniel, Jonathan / Allsport
    Photography USA, Inc.
p. 16—DeFrisco, Tim / Allsport
    Photography USA, Inc.
p. 17—Bello, Al / Allsport
    Photography USA, Inc.
p. 18—Daniel, Jonathan / Allsport
    Photography USA, Inc.

Chapter 4
pp. 19–29—London, Robin G.
p. 30—Perry, Chuck
pp. 31–32—Handelman, Dorothy
p. 33—Perry, Chuck
p. 34, right—Coyle, David
p. 34, left—Perry, Chuck

Chapter 5
pp. 35–38—Perry, Chuck
p. 39—Coyle, David
p. 40—Dunn, Stephen / Allsport
    Photography USA, Inc.
p. 41—Perry, Chuck

Chapter 6
pp. 42–48—Perry, Chuck

Chapter 7
p. 49—Coyle, David
p. 50, left—Perry, Chuck
p. 50, right—Black Box / Index
    Stock Photography, Inc.
pp. 52–55—Seth Poppel Yearbook
    Archives, Inc.

Back Matter
p. 58—London, Robin G.

About the Author

Kieran Scott (first on left) was captain of the 1991 varsity Pascack Hills High School cheerleading squad. After graduating from Rutgers University in 1996, she became an editor and author in New York City. Living in Mahwah, New Jersey, Kieran is still very close with her high school cheerleading friends.